VENUS

MERCURY

SUN

DEDICATED TO THE MEMORIES OF
FRANCES LINCOLN AND LUCY KEELING ✦ JM & CB

First American edition

Kingdom of the Sun copyright © 2001 Frances Lincoln Limited
Text copyright © 2001 Jacqueline Mitton
Illustrations copyright © 2001 Christina Balit

Published by the National Geographic Society.
All rights reserved. Reproduction of the whole or any part of the
contents without written permission from the National Geographic Society
is strictly prohibited.

First published in Great Britain in 2001 by France Lincoln Limited, 4 Torriano
Mews, Torriano Avenue, London NW5 2RZ

Library of Congress Cataloging-in-Publication Data:
Kingdom of the sun : a book of the planets / by Jacqueline Mitton
illustrated by Christina Balit.
p. cm.

ISBN 0-7922-7220-X (Hard Cover)
1. Solar system—Juvenile literature. 2. Gods, Roman—Juvenile
literature. 3. Goddesses, Roman—Juvenile literature. [1. Planets. 2.
Mythology, Roman.] I. Balit, Christina, ill. II. Title.
QB501.3 .M57 2001
523.2—dc21   2001000904

The world's largest nonprofit scientific and educational organization,
the National Geographic Society was founded in 1888 "for the increase
and diffusion of geographic knowledge." Since then it has supported
scientific exploration and spread information to its more than eight
million members worldwide. The Society is supported through member-
ship dues, charitable donations, and income from the sale of its educational products. For more information, please call 1-800-NGS-LINE (647-5463)
or write to the following address:

National Geographic Society
1145 17th Street N.W.
Washington, D.C. 20036-4688
U.S.A.
Visit the Society's Web site:
www.nationalgeographic.com

Printed in Hong Kong

Kingdom of the Sun

A BOOK OF THE PLANETS

JACQUELINE MITTON • CHRISTINA BALIT

NATIONAL GEOGRAPHIC SOCIETY

WASHINGTON, D.C.

WE CAN BE PRETTY SURE that humans have always been sky watchers. Certainly, for many thousands of years people have followed the comings and goings of the Moon and the five brightest planets—the ones we now call Mercury, Venus, Mars, Jupiter, and Saturn.

THE WANDERERS

The English word "planet" comes from the Greek word that means "wanderer." Ancient astronomers counted seven "planets." They included the Sun and Moon because they moved through the constellations. These astronomers also thought that the Earth was at the center, with the seven planets circling around it.

Today, by "planet" we mean a world orbiting the Sun, or any other star. We know that the Moon travels around the Earth, and that the Sun is at the center of a family of nine planets, including the Earth. Three of them were found only after the telescope was invented. Uranus was discovered in 1781, Neptune in 1846, and Pluto in 1930.

CITIZENS OF THE SUN'S KINGDOM

No one really thinks there are more large planets in our Solar System waiting to be discovered, but there are many thousands of miniature planets. More of these are spotted every day. They are called asteroids, or sometimes minor planets.

Most are concentrated in two ring-shaped belts around the Sun. One belt is between the orbits of Mars and Jupiter. The other lies just beyond Neptune and includes Pluto. Altogether, the Sun rules over a huge population.

This book is about the seven celestial "wanderers" known to astronomers in ancient times, along with the three planets discovered since telescopes were invented— all objects that are visible in the night sky from Earth.

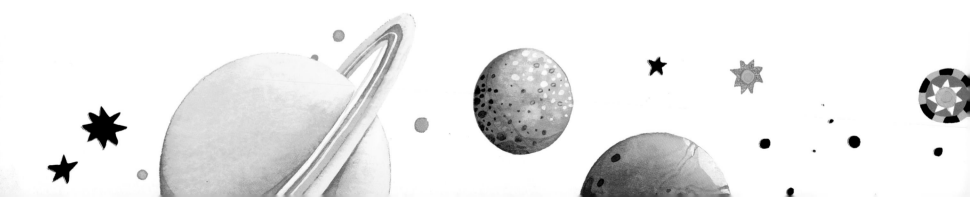

PLANETS AND GODS

About 2,300 years ago, the astronomer Aristotle gave the planets names of Greek gods. He followed the tradition of even earlier Babylonian astronomers who named the planets for their gods. Aristotle did his best to match the character the gods were supposed to have with what he knew about the planets—their speed, brightness, and color.

Later, Greek writing about the planets was translated into the Latin language, so the Greek planet names were changed to the names of the equivalent Roman gods. Hermes became Mercury, Aphrodite became Venus, Ares became Mars, Zeus became Jupiter, and Cronus became Saturn. These are the names that have been handed down to us and are used by astronomers around the world today.

The Greeks also had a god and goddess to personify the Sun and Moon. Their names were Helios and Selene.

NAMING NEW PLANETS

When William Hershel discovered the planet Uranus in 1781, he wanted to name it in honor of the British King George III. In the end, the idea of calling it by the name of another god won out. Uranus was selected because he was the father of Saturn (Cronus) who was the father of Jupiter (Zeus). In one way, the pattern of planet names was broken though. Uranus is a Greek name. It was chosen because there is no Roman equivalent.

The people who first named the planets knew little about them, but modern discoveries link the planets with the old gods in surprising ways. And though our knowledge of the Solar System has increased enormously since the ancient Greeks worshipped their gods, the sense of wonder about the Sun, Moon, and planets is no less than it was all those centuries ago.

THE SUN

A MASSIVE BALL OF GLOWING FLAME, I am sovereign over nine planets. They speed around me along their orbits, trapped by the force of my gravity. Bathed in my rays, their faces beam brightly in the darkness of space.

At dawn I peep above Earth's horizon. I arise and lighten the daytime sky. I climb higher and higher till noon. In ancient Greece, people said I was like a god in a golden chariot, drawn through the heavens by fiery horses. Their name for me was Helios. After sunset they imagined me at rest, making ready for the next day's journey.

But I never rest! Ceaselessly I pour heat and light into the cold empty space around me. For I am a star, a fiery cosmic powerhouse. Billions of years have gone by since I first burst into light. Billions more will pass before I fade and die.

And I sit unmoved at the heart of my kingdom, the Solar System. Meanwhile, Earth spins and circles around me. It is you who are turning. My daily sky-ride is only an illusion.

THE MOON

POCKED WITH CRATERS, pimpled with mountains, my lifeless face is stark and gray. I am no more than a ball of stone, circling the Earth month in and month out. But how do I appear in the clear night sky? I look neither drab nor ugly. Kissed by the rays of the Sun, my somber rock is transformed into beautiful shimmering silver.

Long ago I was seen as a goddess, Selene, sister of Helios, the Sun. Gold and silver, we were a natural pair. His was the bright and cheery day, mine the secret shadowy night. The chariot to carry me through the sky was silver and my horses a pair of purest white.

Night by night, see how my appearance changes. As a slender crescent at dusk, I set soon after the Sun in the west. Within a week, half of me lights the evening hours. Wait seven more days, and my whole round moon-face reflects sunlight over the dark Earth. After two weeks on the wane, I am a crescent once more. My cycle is complete.

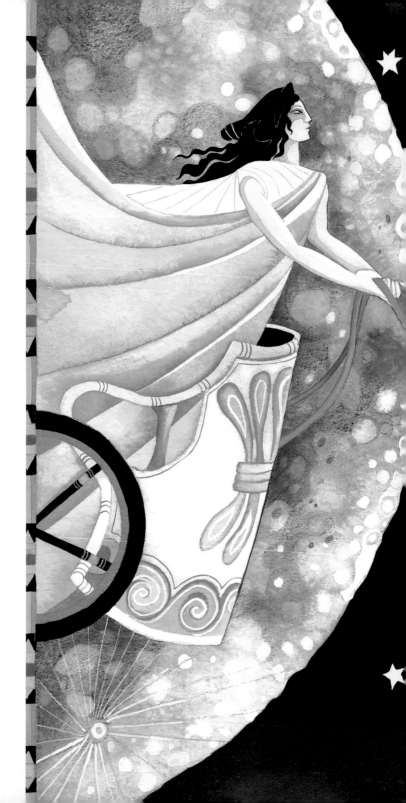

MERCURY

CATCH ME IF YOU CAN as I dash around the Sun! My orbit almost hugs the Sun, and I'm forced to lurk unseen in the dazzle of his brilliance. But now and again, for just a few days, I dodge out of the glare to reveal where I am. And then you might spot me, very low in the twilight sky, shining as brightly as any star.

Swifter in motion than all other planets, I was given the name of Mercury, fleet-footed messenger of the gods and guardian of travelers. So nimble and cunning was he, no one could catch him. With golden-winged sandals upon his feet, he sped over land and sea like a breath of wind.

But no wind stirs on my bleak rocky surface. No atmosphere shields me from the blistering heat. From a pitch black sky, a huge Sun beats down in stillness on a myriad of craters. Then after the Sun has gone down, a desperately chilly night follows the scorching day.

VENUS

A GLITTERING JEWEL OF THE HEAVENS, I blaze like a brilliant diamond. Matchless among the planets, I shine brighter than them all.

And my name I take from the love-goddess Venus, for her wondrous beauty outshone all her rivals. When three goddesses competed to see who was the fairest, she was awarded the prize— a golden apple.

No one could fail to notice her. So when she wished to go unrecognized, she hid her face with a magical sparkling veil.

I, too, have a veil. Silvery cloudtops, glistening brightly in the sunlight, cover me with never a break. No telescope can see my naked face. And so, for many long years, I concealed my secrets.

But then came the spacecraft, armed with probes and radar beams. Now all is revealed. Fiery volcanoes have molded features into my face unlike anything else in the Solar System. My atmosphere weighs down with almost incredible force. My world is seared by sweltering heat.

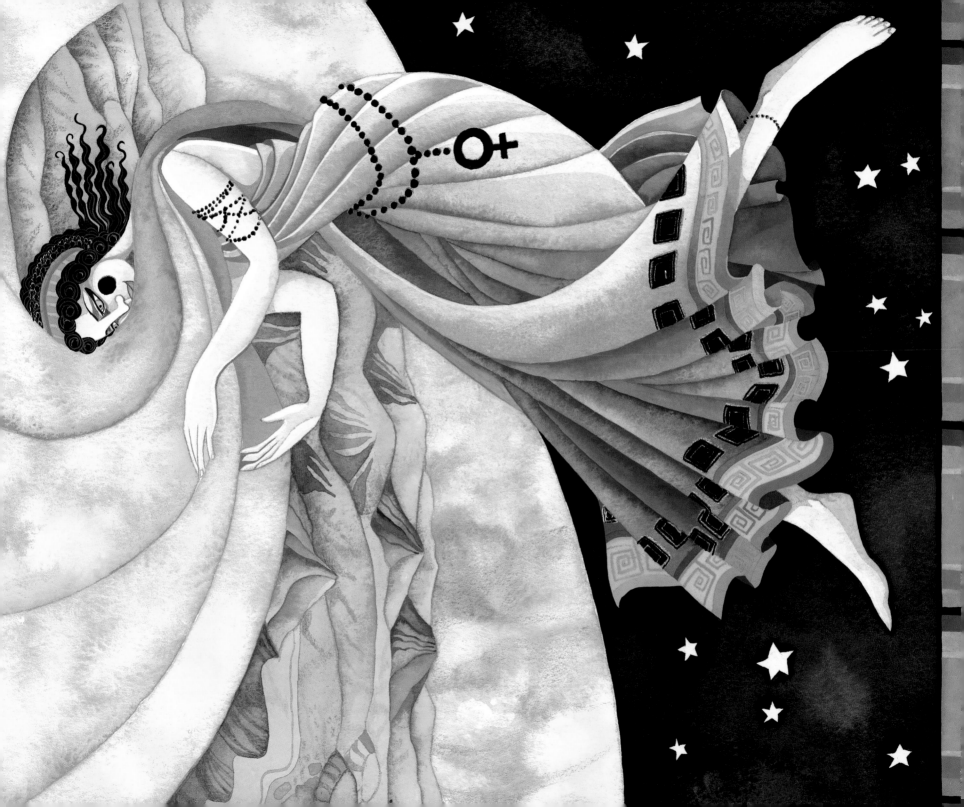

MARS

LIKE A FLAMING RUBY I burn in the night sky. They call me the Red Planet. Mine is the color for anger and danger—the color of blood.

Mars is the name I share with the god of war. Most feared of the gods, he was furious and fickle. He gloried in fighting and bloodshed. Fear and Terror were his constant companions. They follow me too, for my two tiny moons bear those names as the ancient Greeks would have said them—Phobos and Deimos.

But in truth I am a small and unthreatening world. My seasons come and go as on Earth. My only fury is the wind that blows wild and whips up rust-red dust till it fills the thin air and billows for mile upon mile. Travel back in time, though, and you would see me differently. Towering volcanoes, long since extinct, are silent witnesses to my violent past. Winding channels scar me where torrents of water once swept by. But that was billions of years ago. Dry, shifting sand is all that moves on Mars today.

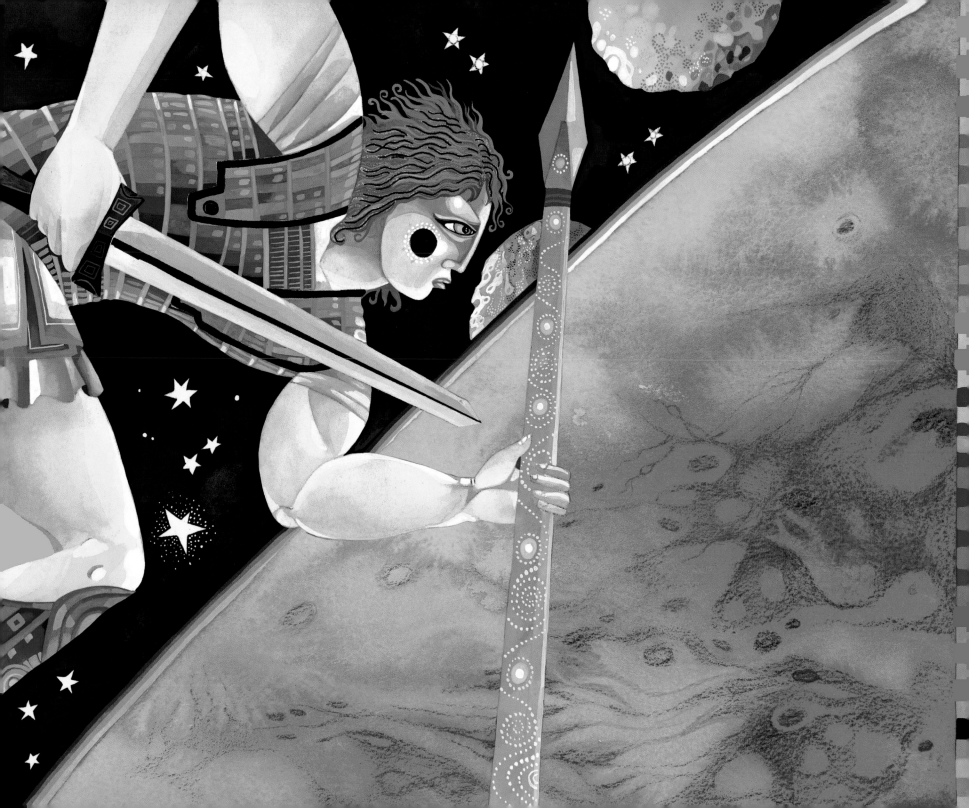

JUPITER

I AM THE GREATEST of the Sun's planets. My bulk surpasses a thousand Earths. My radiance makes me a beacon of the night—brilliant, yellow, and steadfast. A retinue of twenty-eight moons or more revolves around me, caught in my gravity's power.

It is fitting that I am called Jupiter, named for the greatest of the gods who ruled supreme among them all. Clouds and rain were his special charge, thunder and lightning signs of his anger.

Clouds are my glory, too, swirling, whirling, and weaving intricate patterns. And flashing through my stormy weather, immense electric sparks inject my clouds with jagged lightning. My most enormous storm of all has raged for hundreds of years, spiralling wildly. Called the Great Red Spot, it could cover several Earths.

Plunge below my restless kaleidoscope of clouds, and you would find an unimaginably strange world where thick gas blends little by little into liquid. Venture deeper into my globe, and encounter a metallic liquid like nothing known on Earth.

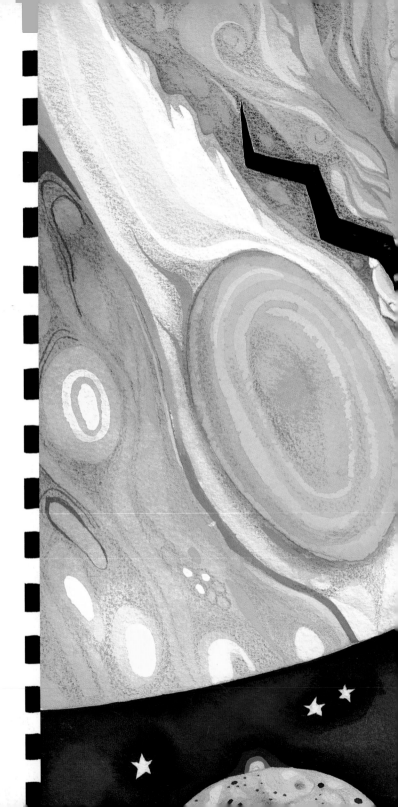

SATURN

WHAT A GLORIOUS ARRAY of rings and moons surrounds me! I preside over a wealth of plenty, as did Saturn the god. My rings are shoals of countless scurrying moonlets, casting a multicolored girdle around my belly. Braiding and streaming, clustering here, dividing there, they whirl by in a frenzy. Some are icy boulders the size of castles. The smallest are mere specks of dust. My main moons—those large enough to have their own names—number at least thirty.

My namesake among the gods was once ruler of them all. But he yielded to Jupiter, his mightier son, who banished him far into the heavens. Indeed, I am almost double Jupiter's distance from the Sun. By size I rank a close second to him.

A veil of haze makes my creamy clouds look calm. But things are not always as they seem. High-speed winds race around my spinning globe. Now and then, a giant storm breaks out, topped by a dramatic white cloud.

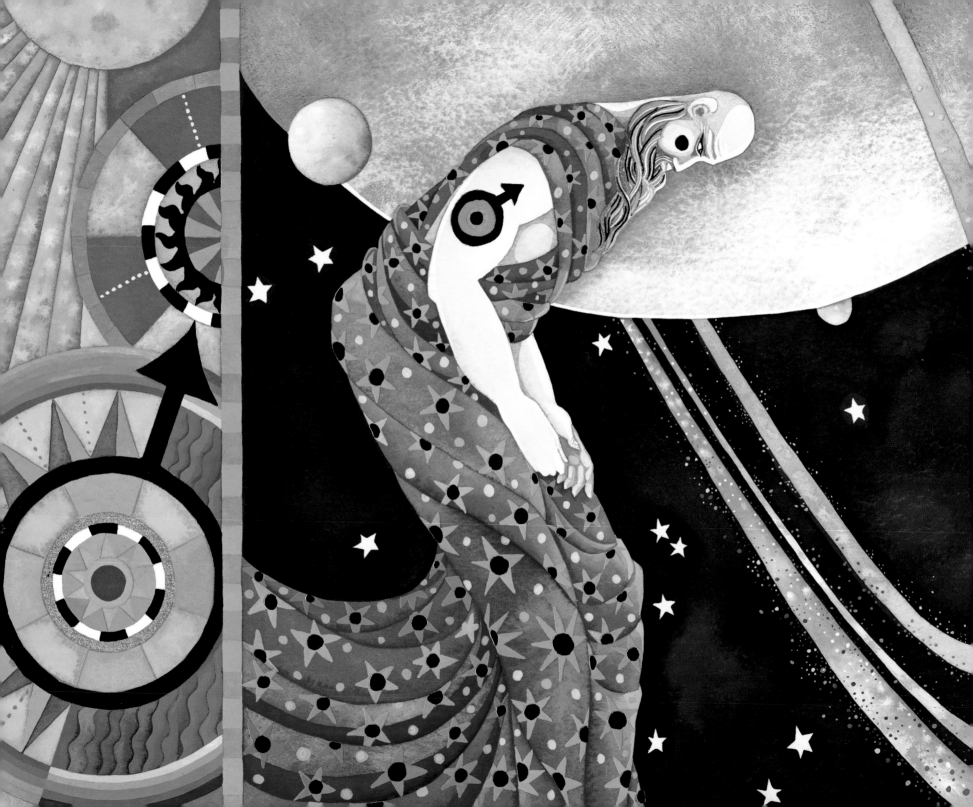

URANUS

AN ORB OF PALE AND GENTLE BLUE, with scarcely a feature to show, I wend my way around the Sun in the distant reaches of the Solar System. With my heavenly color, I am fittingly named for the sky god of old. Husband of Mother Earth, for he was father to Saturn, and Jupiter was his grandson.

Set four Earths side by side to gauge my size. Though I have a rocky core, my main bulk is a curious chemical sea, with a hazy atmosphere above. Clouds are rare, and I am indeed plain and bland. Some declare me dull. Yet I have a little mystery. As I voyage on my path through space, I roll along upon my side, axis askew. What happened in the dim and distant past to cause me to tumble so?

A swarm of little moons buzzes around me. Astronomers have counted twenty-one. My nine fine rings of flying boulders are dim and dark— dark as anything in the Sun's whole realm.

NEPTUNE

THROUGH THE DEPTHS OF SPACE, I sail my course around the Sun, six times farther out than Jupiter. My face is bright blue, the color of Earth's ocean. My name I take from the god of the seas, Jupiter's powerful, bad-tempered brother. With a shake of his three-pronged trident he could summon a storm at will. And he rode the surf in a chariot pulled by magical serpent horses.

Like the white foam horses atop tumbling waves, ice-crystal clouds form glistening froth upon me. They gallop along, tossed by the fiercest winds known on any planet, then they vanish into the blue. Once in a while, brooding storms blow up in writhing oval spots of darker hue.

Though I am named for Jupiter's brother, by nature Uranus is my closest kin. Like him I'm surrounded by thin dusky rings, though one of mine is a broken chain of curving arcs. We are a pair of blue giants, but Uranus is serene while I am wild and tempestuous.

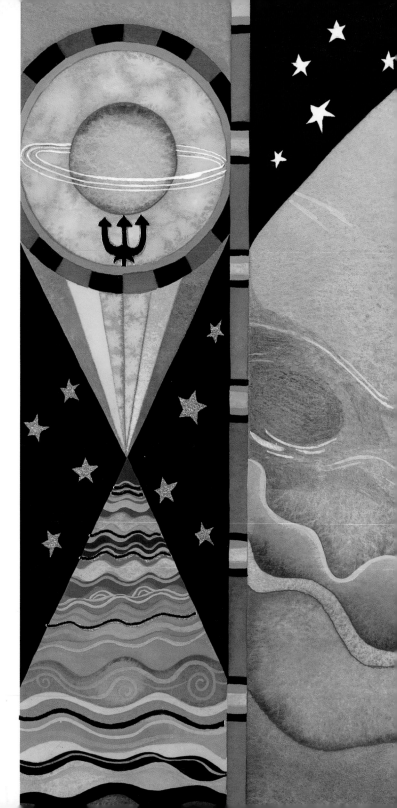

PLUTO

AT THE FAR-FLUNG EDGE of the Sun's domain, chilled almost to the deepest cold that ever can be, I hold my moon, Charon, close. Two miniature worlds of ice and rock, we circle each other face-to-face. The sunbeams that reach me are weak after traveling so very far. Darkness envelops us, like the gloom in the caverns of the underworld where Pluto the god reigned. His was the realm of the souls of the dead, and Charon was the boatman who ferried them there.

All around me, thousands of icy bodies wander through space like ghosts. These dwarf planets accompany me on centuries-long loops around the Solar System, where Neptune lies and beyond. My oval course sometimes swings me as near as Neptune, sometimes carries me much farther off. Because I am so far away and tiny—less than one fifth of Earth's span—vague shadowy patches are all that can be seen of me, though telescopes strain their best. No spacecraft has yet been my way to snatch a close-up of my face.

MORE ABOUT THE SUN, MOON AND PLANETS

PLANET NAME	AVERAGE DISTANCE FROM SUN	DIAMETER AT EQUATOR	TIME TO ORBIT SUN	NUMBER OF MOONS
MERCURY	36 million miles (58 million km)	3,031 miles (4,878 km)	88.0 days	0
VENUS	67 million miles (108 million km)	7,521 miles (12,104 km)	224.7 days	0
EARTH	93 million miles (150 million km)	7,926 miles (12,756 km)	1.00 year	1
MARS	142 million miles (228 million km)	4,222 miles (6,794 km)	1.88 years	2
JUPITER	483 million miles (778 million km)	89,408 miles (143,884 km)	11.86 years	28
SATURN	887 million miles (1,427 million km)	74,898 miles (120,536 km)	29.46 years	30
URANUS	1,784 million miles (2,871 million km)	31,765 miles (51,118 km)	84.01 years	21
NEPTUNE	2,794 million miles (4,497 million km)	4,222 miles (6,794 km)	164.79 years	8
PLUTO	3,675 million miles (5,914 million km)	1,466 miles (2,360 km)	248 years	1

Mercury, Venus, and Mars are small rocky planets like Earth. The Moon is like a small rocky planet too. The four giant planets—Jupiter, Saturn, Uranus, and Neptune—have rocky cores, but there is no solid surface below their atmospheres. Instead, the gas gets thicker the farther you go down until it merges into a very deep layer of liquid. Tiny Pluto is different again, made of a mixture of ice and rock.

ABOUT THE SUN

- 109 times larger than Earth
- 333,000 times more massive than Earth
- 27 million °F (15 million °C) at the center
- 10,000 °F (5,500 °C) at the surface

ABOUT THE MOON

- Diameter 2,160 miles (3,476 km)
- Average distance from Earth 238,861 miles (384,400 km)
- Takes 27.32 Earth days to spin once
- There are 29.53 days between new Moons

GLOSSARY

ASTRONOMER – Someone who studies the universe and the things in it, such as stars and planets.

ATMOSPHERE – A layer of gas around a moon, planet, or star.

CONSTELLATION – A named area of sky and the pattern of stars in it.

COSMIC – To do with space or the universe.

CRATER – A bowl-shaped hole in the surface of a moon or planet.

GRAVITY – A natural force that makes objects attract each other.

HORIZON – Where the sky seems to meet the ground.

MOON – A body that moves in orbit around a planet.

MOONLET – A very small moon.

ORBIT – The path in space of one body around another; to travel around another body.

PLANET – A world that travels around a star and that, unlike a star, is not massive enough to give out any light of its own.

PROBE – A spacecraft sent to investigate the atmosphere or surface of a planet or moon, by dropping through the atmosphere or landing on the surface.

RADAR – A way of finding out the distance to something by bouncing radio waves from it.

SOLAR SYSTEM – All the things in orbit around the Sun that are kept there by the Sun's gravity, including the planets with their moons, comets, and asteroids.

STAR – A large glowing ball of hot gas.

VOLCANO – A mountain formed where molten rock has welled up to the surface from the inside of a planet.

RELATIVE SIZES OF
THE GIANT PLANETS

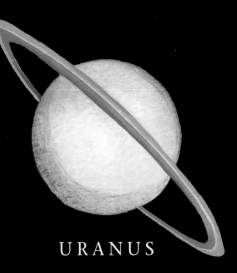

URANUS

SIZE OF EARTH

|————————————————————|

80,000 km; 50,000 miles

JUPITER